PHOTOGRAPHIC MEMORIES OF BRITAIN

PEAK DISTRICT

Roly Smith, president of the Outdoor Writers' Guild and member of the British Guild of Travel Writers, is a freelance writer and editor, and the author of over 30 books on walking and the countryside. Based in Bakewell in the Peak District, Roly took voluntary early retirement from his position as Head of Information Services with the Peak District National Park in May 1997, to concentrate on his freelance career. Previously he enjoyed a 20-year, award-winning career in daily paper journalism, latterly on the *Birmingham Post* and *Evening Mail*. He is vice president of the South Yorkshire and North East Derbyshire area of the Ramblers' Association.

PHOTOGRAPHIC MEMORIES
OF BRITAIN

PHOTOGRAPHIC MEMORIES OF BRITAIN

PEAK DISTRICT

ROLY SMITH

FRITH
BOOK Co

First published in the United Kingdom in 2003 by
Frith Book Company Ltd

Hardback Edition 2003
ISBN 1-85937-786-6

British Library Cataloguing in Publication Data

Photographic Memories of Britain - Peak District
Roly Smith

Frith Book Company Ltd
Frith's Barn, Teffont,
Salisbury, Wiltshire SP3 5QP
Tel: +44 (0) 1722 716 376
Email: info@francisfrith.co.uk
www.francisfrith.co.uk

Printed and bound in Great Britain

Front Cover: **CASTLETON,** *Bargate 1932* *85233*
Frontispiece: **HADDON HALL,** *c1870* *5229*

The following images were supplied by Karen Frenkel:
M350701 (Page 27), M47701 (Page 32), C72701 (Page 62)
T46701 (Page 79), B263702 (Page 94), B263701 (Page 95)

AS WITH ANY HISTORICAL DATABASE THE FRITH ARCHIVE IS CONSTANTLY BEING CORRECTED AND IMPROVED AND THE PUBLISHERS WOULD WELCOME INFORMATION ON OMISSIONS OR INACCURACIES

CONTENTS

FRANCIS FRITH

VICTORIAN PIONEER

FRANCIS FRITH, founder of the world-famous photographic archive, was a complex and multi-talented man. A devout Quaker and a highly successful Victorian businessman, he was philosophic by nature and pioneering in outlook.

By 1855 he had already established a wholesale grocery business in Liverpool, and sold it for the astonishing sum of £200,000, which is the equivalent today of over £15,000,000. Now a very rich man, he was able to indulge his passion for travel. As a child he had pored over travel books written by early explorers, and his fancy and imagination had been stirred by family holidays to the sublime mountain regions of Wales and Scotland. 'What lands of spirit-stirring and enriching scenes and places!' he had written. He was to return to these scenes of grandeur in later years to 'recapture the thousands of vivid and tender memories', but with a different purpose. Now in his thirties, and captivated by the new science of photography, Frith set out on a series of pioneering journeys up the Nile and to the Near East that occupied him from 1856 until 1860.

INTRIGUE AND EXPLORATION

These far-flung journeys were packed with intrigue and adventure. In his life story, written when he was sixty-three, Frith tells of being held captive by bandits, and of fighting 'an awful midnight battle to the very point of surrender with a deadly pack of hungry, wild dogs'. Wearing flowing Arab costume, Frith arrived at Akaba by camel seventy years before Lawrence of Arabia, where he encountered 'desert princes and rival sheikhs, blazing with jewel-hilted swords'.

He was the first photographer to venture beyond the sixth cataract of the Nile. Africa was still the mysterious 'Dark Continent', and Stanley and Livingstone's historic meeting was a decade into the future. The conditions for picture taking confound belief. He laboured for hours in his wicker dark-room in the sweltering heat of the desert, while the volatile chemicals fizzed dangerously in their trays. Back in London he exhibited his photographs and was 'rapturously cheered' by members of the Royal Society. His reputation as a photographer was made overnight.

VENTURE OF A LIFE-TIME

Characteristically, Frith quickly spotted the opportunity to create a new business as a specialist publisher of photographs. He lived in an era of immense and sometimes violent change.

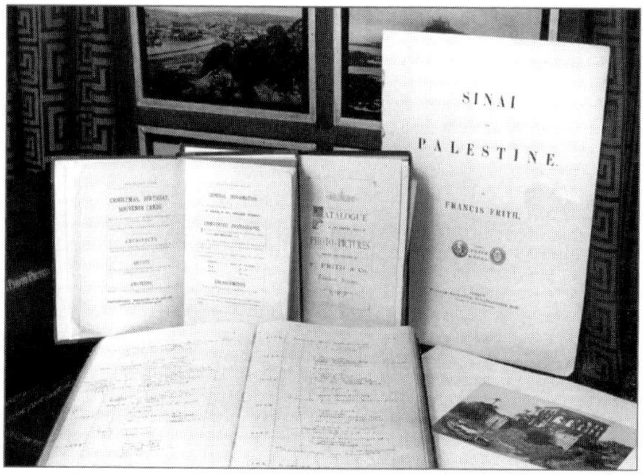

For the poor in the early part of Victoria's reign work was exhausting and the hours long, and people had precious little free time to enjoy themselves. Most had no transport other than a cart or gig at their disposal, and rarely travelled far beyond the boundaries of their own town or village. However, by the 1870s the railways had threaded their way across the country, and Bank Holidays and half-day Saturdays had been made obligatory by Act of Parliament. All of a sudden the working man and his family were able to enjoy days out and see a little more of the world.

With typical business acumen, Francis Frith foresaw that these new tourists would enjoy having souvenirs to commemorate their days out. In 1860 he married Mary Ann Rosling and set out on a new career: his aim was to photograph every city, town and village in Britain. For the next thirty years he travelled the country by train and by pony and trap, producing fine photographs of seaside resorts and beauty spots that were keenly bought by millions of Victorians. These prints were painstakingly pasted into family albums and pored over during the dark nights of winter, rekindling precious memories of summer excursions.

THE RISE OF FRITH & CO

Frith's studio was soon supplying retail shops all over the country. To meet the demand he gathered about him a small team of photographers, and published the work of independent artist-photographers of the calibre of Roger Fenton and Francis Bedford. In order to gain some understanding of the scale of Frith's business one only has to look at the catalogue issued by Frith & Co in 1886: it runs to some 670 pages, listing not only many thousands of views of the British Isles but also many photographs of most European countries, and China, Japan, the USA and Canada - note the sample page shown on page 9 from the hand-written Frith & Co ledgers recording the pictures. By 1890 Frith had created the greatest specialist photographic publishing company in the world, with over 2,000 sales outlets - more than the combined number that Boots and WH Smith have today! The picture on the next page shows the Frith & Co display board at Ingleton in the Yorkshire Dales (left of window). Beautifully constructed with a mahogany frame and gilt inserts, it could display up to a dozen local scenes.

POSTCARD BONANZA

The ever-popular holiday postcard we know today took many years to develop. In 1870 the Post Office issued the first plain cards, with a pre-printed stamp on one face. In 1894 they allowed other publishers' cards to be sent through the mail with an attached adhesive half-penny stamp. Demand grew rapidly, and in 1895 a new size of postcard was permitted called the court card, but there was little room for illustration. In 1899, a year after Frith's death, a new card measuring 5.5 x 3.5 inches became the standard format, but it was not until 1902 that the divided back came into being, so that the address and message could be on one face and a full-size illustration on the other. Frith & Co were in the vanguard of postcard development: Frith's sons Eustace and Cyril continued their father's monumental task, expanding the number of views offered to the public and recording more

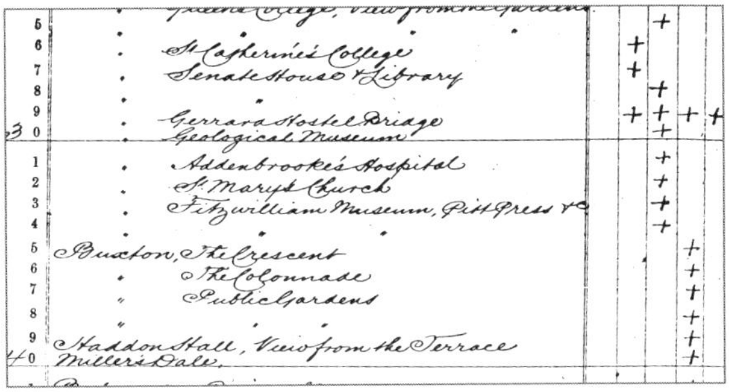

6 St Catherine's College
7 Senate House & Library
8
9 Gerrard Hostel Bridge
30 Geological Museum
1 Addenbrooke's Hospital
2 St Mary's Church
3 Fitzwilliam Museum, Pitt Press &c
4
5 Buxton, The Crescent
6 The Colonnade
7 Public Gardens
8
9 Haddon Hall, View from the Terrace
40 Millers Dale

and more places in Britain, as the coasts and countryside were opened up to mass travel.

Francis Frith had died in 1898 at his villa in Cannes, his great project still growing. The archive he created continued in business for another seventy years. By 1970 it contained over a third of a million pictures showing 7,000 British towns and villages.

FRANCIS FRITH'S LEGACY

Frith's legacy to us today is of immense significance and value, for the magnificent archive of evocative photographs he created provides a unique record of change in the cities, towns and villages throughout Britain over a century and more. Frith and his fellow studio photographers revisited locations many times down the years to update their views, compiling for us an enthralling and colourful pageant of British life and character.

We are fortunate that Frith was dedicated to recording the minutiae of everyday life. For it is this sheer wealth of visual data, the painstaking chronicle of changes in dress, transport, street layouts, buildings, housing, engineering and landscape that captivates us so much today. His remarkable images offer us a powerful link with the past and with the lives of our ancestors.

THE VALUE OF THE ARCHIVE TODAY

Computers have now made it possible for Frith's many thousands of images to be accessed almost instantly. Frith's images are increasingly used as visual resources, by social historians, by researchers into genealogy and ancestry, by architects and town planners, and by teachers involved in local history projects.

In addition, the archive offers every one of us an opportunity to examine the places where we and our families have lived and worked down the years. Highly successful in Frith's own era, the archive is now, a century and more on, entering a new phase of popularity. Historians consider the Francis Frith Collection to be of prime national importance. It is the only archive of its kind remaining in private ownership. Francis Frith's archive is now housed in an historic timber barn in the beautiful village of Teffont in Wiltshire. Its founder would not recognize the archive office as it is today. In place of the many thousands of dusty boxes containing glass plate negatives and an all-pervading odour of photographic chemicals, there are now ranks of computer screens. He would be amazed to watch his images travelling round the world at unimaginable speeds through internet lines.

The archive's future is both bright and exciting. Francis Frith, with his unshakeable belief in making photographs available to the greatest number of people, would undoubtedly approve of what is being done today with his lifetime's work. His photographs depicting our shared past are now bringing pleasure and enlightenment to millions around the world a century and more after his death.

PEAK DISTRICT
AN INTRODUCTION

THE Peak District, the last vertebra in the stony backbone of England, is an area full of paradoxes. Despite the name, there are few hills which really justify the name 'peak.' The name originates from the Old English 'peac', which meant 'knoll' or 'hill', and did not have the modern dictionary meaning of 'a sharply pointed summit'. In fact, the most common view in the Peak is a perspective of horizontal plateaux.

Another Peak District paradox is the name 'low,' so common on Peak District maps. There are 70 of these on the limestone White Peak plateau alone, and almost without exception, they mark a hill or a high point in the landscape. The confusing name also comes from an Old English word – 'hlaw' – which meant 'burial mound' or 'hill', and usually denotes a tumulus dating from the Bronze Age. So where you see 'low' in the Peak District, it usually denotes a high place.

History shows us that the Peak has always been a place set apart from the rest of Britain. Its earliest-known named inhabitants were the Saxon tribe known as the Pecsaetan, the 'people of the Peak' – a separate and independent tribe from the Mercians, who ruled much of central England during the Dark Ages. This apartness is echoed in the many strange and often unique ancient customs and legends which have lived on in the limestone and gritstone hills of the Peak, long after they have disappeared elsewhere in Britain. Examples of these which are still practiced are the ancient, originally pagan, custom of well-dressing, and the mysterious Castleton Garland Ceremony, which was perhaps instituted as a pagan celebration of the return of spring.

There are two quite distinct types of scenery in the Peak District, imparting contrasting, almost male and female, characteristics to the landscape. These very different landscapes have been given the names Dark Peak and White Peak, and have been widely adopted now, even on Ordnance Survey maps. The physical relationship between the Dark Peak and White Peak is perhaps best described by imagining a man's balding head. The remaining 'hair' can be seen as the Dark Peak moors to the north, east and west, leaving the 'skin' of the central limestone plateau of the White Peak exposed in the middle and south.

The Dark Peak is the name given to the northern, eastern and western millstone grit moorlands of the Peak District. This is a macho terrain, consisting of dark, brooding tablelands punctuated by steep, rocky valleys known as cloughs; weird, wind-carved tors or towers of rock; and moorlands bordered by steep walls of naked rock, known as 'edges.' The moors are dominated by heather, bilberry and moor grass, but on the highest points, such as Kinder Scout, Bleaklow and Black Hill, years of over-grazing, acid rain and natural erosion have robbed the soil of vegetation, and left behind only the dark and dank peat bogs. Settlements here are usually isolated villages, sheltering in the dales beneath the moors, although some of the larger towns, like Buxton, Chapel-en-le-Frith and Leek, are also found on the edge of the Dark Peak moors.

Although both the limestone and the millstone grit were formed during the same Carboniferous period about 350 million years ago, the pale limestone of the White Peak is the older of the two rocks. It lies beneath the gritstone moors and edges, but it has been exposed by centuries of uplifting and erosion into the Derbyshire Dome, that 'bald patch' which is the 1,000ft (300m) central limestone plateau, dissected by distinctive, steep-sided dales.

The White Peak is an altogether more gentle, feminine kind of landscape than the Dark Peak. The swelling contours of the limestone plateau are covered by a network of dry stone walls – a feature of the Peak District which often makes the most lasting impression on first-time visitors, especially those coming from the south. Most of these characteristic walls are about 200 years old, built at the time of the Parliamentary Enclosure Movements of the 18th and 19th centuries, but some have recently been dated to as early as Romano-British times. The most important prehistoric remains, such as the stone circle and henge of Arbor Low and the Five Wells chambered tomb at Taddington, for example, are also found high on the limestone plateau, where villages like Tideswell and Monyash shelter in shallow depressions, usually around the village pond or 'mere.'

Most of the White Peak dales are too narrow to accommodate a road, and therefore they are almost exclusively the preserve of walkers. Over the years, but especially since the turn of the century (as we can see from the photographs in this collection), they have come in their thousands to enjoy the scenic splendour of places like Dovedale, Monsal Dale and Lathkill Dale.

The broad, well-wooded and fertile shale valleys of the Derwent and the Wye – the Peak's two major rivers – are where many of the Peak District's larger settlements, such as Bakewell and the Matlocks, lie. The shale valleys are also where the local aristocracy built the famous stately homes of the Peak, such as Chatsworth, home of the Duke of Devonshire, on the Derwent near Baslow, and the Duke of Rutland's Haddon Hall, standing on a bluff above the River Wye near Bakewell.

Buxton is by far the biggest town in the Peak District, and where most of its visitors have traditionally stayed, but it only really came to prominence during the 18th century. The 5th Duke of Devonshire used some of the enormous profits he made from his copper and lead mines at Ecton Hill in Staffordshire on a grand building spree which attempted to make Buxton a rival to Bath as a fashionable spa. Buildings like John Carr's splendid Crescent, the Natural Baths and St Ann's Well serve to remind the visitor of that briefly successful venture, which received its final boost from the coming of the Midland Railway – it was engineered through the hills of the Peak in 1863.

The tepid spring waters of Buxton also attracted the Romans into the forbidding hills of the Peak District, and they named the town Aqua Arnemetiae. But the chief reason for the Roman expansion into the Peak was the abundant supplies of lead ore in the limestone strata of the White Peak. The Romans were the first to commercially exploit the Peak's lead riches, but the lead mining industry reached its zenith during the 18th and 19th centuries. At this time almost every White Peak farmer doubled as a lead miner and operated in a true dual economy.

Bakewell is the unofficial capital of the Peak District, but it still has a population of only 4,000 people. Founded by the Saxons, the town has commanded an important crossing of the Wye for well over 1,000 years, and was first awarded a grant for a weekly market in 1254. That market still takes place on a Monday, but no longer in the street in front of the Rutland Arms – birthplace of the traditional delicacy, the Bakewell pudding – but in the new Agricultural and Business Centre next to the Bakewell showground across the river.

Another of the major 'honeypots' of the Peak District both in these early photographs and also still today is Castleton, the township at the head of the Hope Valley. Castleton grew up as a planned settlement in the shadow of William Peveril's castle, lording it on its crag between the gorge of Peak Cavern and Cave Dale. It is probably most famous for its four show caverns, formed at the junction of the limestone with the gritstone, which have attracted visitors since the days of Daniel Defoe and Queen Victoria.

The other stone-built villages in the Peak have hardly changed since Francis Frith first took his camera there at the end of the 19th century, as many of the following photographs show.

Perhaps the greatest change has been in the different forms of transport we see. Horses and carts were gradually superseded by motor vehicles, and children could no longer play in the street as the ancient peace of the dales was shattered by the transport revolution.

The Peak District became the first National Park in Britain just over half a century ago in April 1951. It stood out then as the last unspoilt open space between Manchester and Sheffield and the rest of the great conurbations of northern and central England. The populations of those surrounding cities had long used the Peak for their weekend recreation, as Frith's earliest photographs show well. But by the Fifties, the creeping suburbia, roadside signs and the red-brick villas of the fast-expanding cities were insidiously creeping out towards the hills of the Peak, unchecked by any planning restrictions.

The proximity to the huge populations of the Midlands and north – half the population of England lives within 60 miles of the Peak District – has inevitably led to problems of congestion in recent years. It has been claimed that the 22 million day visits to the Peak District National Park make it the second most visited National Park in the world, and the narrow Peakland roads and paths often show signs of serious congestion and wear and tear.

But this new collection of photographs from Frith's unique archive shows us what the Peak District was like before the impact of mass tourism of today really took hold. We start our 'Frith's Tour' in the limestone dales of the south, beginning with Dovedale and Matlock, moving north to the Wye Valley and the villages around Bakewell and then to the central limestone area up to the Hope Valley. Then we turn east to the villages which fringe the edges of the Derwent Valley, and then west to Buxton and the gritstone area of the Staffordshire and Cheshire moorlands. Finally, we look at the towns and villages below the moors of the Dark Peak in the far north of the area.

The challenge which faces the Peak District National Park today is to continue to safeguard and protect this precious resource so that future generations can continue to enjoy its amazingly unspoilt beauty.

THE SOUTH

MILLDALE
The Village c1955 M394006

The hamlet of Milldale marks the end of the five-mile walk through the lower reaches of Dovedale, and is endlessly popular with walkers. This view shows a party of ramblers inspecting their maps outside the teashop in the centre of the hamlet.

ASHBOURNE
The Church 1896
37873

The novelist George Eliot famously described the beautiful cruciform parish church of St Oswald in Ashbourne as 'the finest mere parish church in England'. Its stately 212ft-high Decorated spire, seen here from the south, is the tallest in the Peak District, but the mainly 13th- and 14th-century church was heavily restored in 1886.

ASHBOURNE, *Market Place 1957* A66018

Ashbourne was first recorded as holding a market in 1257, 24 years before the town became a borough, and the triangular, sloping Market Place is still the venue for the weekly event every Saturday. This view looks up the market towards the porticoed Town Hall in the centre of the photograph.

BONSALL
Via Gellia,
The Pig of Lead Inn
1892 31300

Note the horse and cart on the left of the Pig of Lead Inn, and the man standing in the middle of the street with what appears to be harness for a horse. On the right, a smartly-suited man watches over a baby in a pram, while two sailor-suited boys look on (centre). The inn's name recalls the days when the village was an important centre in the lead mining industry of the White Peak.

▼ **BONSALL,** *The Church c1960* B485002

The parish church of St James overlooks the former lead mining village from its hilltop site. It dates mainly from the 14th century, and its fine tower and spire is surmounted by stone crowns and gargoyles.

► **BONSALL**
The Cross c1960
B485302

Bonsall's 17th-century market cross is set into the hillside of its steeply-sloping Market Square. Bonsall, just off the Via Gellia near Cromford, was famous as a lead mining village, and the King's Head Inn, to the left in the background of this photograph, dates from 1677 and is said to be haunted. The former village store in the background is now a private house.

◄ **BRASSINGTON**
General View of the Village c1960
B487015

Brassington lies in the heart of the White Peak lead mining country, and there are many reminders of the work of 't'owd man' – as the lead miners were called – in the surrounding fields. This photograph shows a view of the limestone cottages of the village from the south.

► **BRASSINGTON**
Harboro' Rocks c1960 B487014

Harboro' Rocks is an interesting outcrop of dolomitic limestone which has been affected by great heat to become more porous than the surrounding Carboniferous limestone of the White Peak. The pock-marked limestone creates this distinctive landscape of upstanding tors.

CROMFORD
Willersley Castle From the South c1955 C193288

The mock-Gothic Willersley Castle was built by Richard Arkwright (the great industrialist and inventor of the water-powered spinning frame) between 1782 and 1788 as his mansion and family home. Unfortunately, he never lived there: the castle was burnt down in 1791, and he died before it was rebuilt and finished. His son, however, lived there, and it later became a Methodist guest house.

CROMFORD, *The Bridge 1886* 18578

This photograph of the 15th-century Cromford Bridge shows a shadowy black-coated figure in the foreground fishing in the River Derwent. This view is from the downstream side of the bridge, where the arches are pointed, whereas on the upstream side, they are rounded. A stone on the bridge marks the spot where Benjamin Heywood went straight into the river as he returned home on horseback in 1697, and emerged unscathed.

CROMFORD
Black Rocks c1960
C193013

Cromford Black Rocks, seen here from below on the line of the Cromford and High Peak Railway (now the High Peak Trail), is a favourite place for rock climbers. It was first explored by pioneers such as J W Puttrell of Sheffield, and it was later developed by Manchester climbers such as Joe Brown and Don Whillans.

CROMFORD, *Black Rocks 1892* 31294

The overhanging, topmost rocks of the Black Rocks, showing many instances of graffiti, some of which is Victorian, defacing the gritstone boulders – notice the examples in the foreground. There is a fine view across the Derwent Valley from here across towards Matlock and Riber Castle.

DOVEDALE, *Reynard's Cave 1914* 67604

A picnic party decamps on the banks of the Dove below Reynard's Cave, the natural arch of limestone which can be seen in the upper left of this photograph. The 'cave', formed by differential erosion of the limestone, is one of the many rock formations which attract tourists to Dovedale.

DOVEDALE, *Reynard's Cave from Above c1864* 2087

Looking down from the cave towards the river. The cave was the scene of a tragedy in 1761 when the Rev Dean Langton attempted to climb the steep slope into the cave on horseback, but his horse slipped on the scree and he was thrown off and killed. The incident is commemorated by a plaque in Ashbourne church.

◀ DOVEDALE
c1960 D145006

Walkers start the climb up to Lover's Leap in the first section of the walk from the Stepping Stones through Dovedale. On the left we can see the limestone spires of the Twelve Apostles peeping through the trees, one of the many rock features in the dale which were given fanciful names by the Victorians.

DOVEDALE
Lion Rock 1899
34261

With a little imagination, the noble profile of a lion's head can be seen on the part of the lovely riverside walk through Dovedale known as the Narrows. The path, one of the most popular in the Peak District National Park, is now duck-boarded on this section, where the river often floods in the winter.

DOVEDALE, *Ilam Hall Caravan Site c1960* D145074

Ilam Hall was built by the shipping magnate, Jesse Watts Russell, in a high Gothic battlemented style in 1828, but it was partly demolished in 1934 and became a youth hostel, now leased from the National Trust. This view shows the caravan site which existed on the site in the 1960s, with the wooded slopes of Dovedale beyond.

ELTON
The Post Office and the Church c1950
E131013a

Elton is a typical White Peak village founded on the dual economies of farming and lead mining, and there are many fine 18th-century houses in the village street, some of which we can see here. The pinnacled tower of the parish church of All Saints, reconstructed after a steeple collapse in 1812, rises on the left.

▼ MATLOCK, *Riber Castle and the River Derwent c1955* M273061

A romantic view of John Smedley's fairy-tale Riber Castle, seen from the River Derwent. The castle, which was built in 1862 with Smedley as sole architect, was never fully completed, though Smedley's wife continued to live there after he died. It has had a chequered history, serving as a zoo and wildlife park before the current plans to convert it for housing. John Smedley had a big influence on Matlock; he was the owner of its largest hydropathic establishment, and built six churches.

► MATLOCK BANK
1892 31291

Eight former hamlets with Matlock in their name make up the present town of Matlock, and as the name suggests, Matlock Bank spreads up the eastern bank of the Derwent. A mill chimney is prominent in the picture to the left, while in the background is Smedley's Hydropathic Establishment at Matlock, providing a popular cure for all sorts of ills.

◄ **MATLOCK BATH**
1886 18592

This is a very early view of Matlock Bath, taken before the tourism invasion made it a sort of inland Blackpool, much loved by leather-clad motorcyclists. The main Derby-Bakewell road, now the A6, winds through the picture, while behind the church, rows of allotments go up the hillside in an area which is today covered by houses. The River Derwent is on the left.

► **MATLOCK BANK**
1999 M350701

This photograph was taken from an almost identical position to No 31291 over a century later. Smedley's Hydro still dominates this view of Matlock, although today it has a new use as the administrative headquarters of Derbyshire County Council. The mill chimney on the left has gone, and houses and shops now spread up Bank Road, to the right of the photograph, in addition to filling the foreground and the area in front of the county offices.

MATLOCK BATH
Derwent Terrace c1864
2094

This view shows the spire of the chapel in the centre of the picture. Rows of houses and hotels are lined up along the bank of the River Derwent, and the green limestone hills rise beyond.

▶ **MATLOCK BATH**
Main Street 1892
31274

This view up the main street, now the A6, at Matlock Bath is interesting because it shows the wooded slopes above before the construction of the Heights of Abraham Prospect Tower, now the terminus of the cable car ride. The Royal Museum, now gone, is on the right, and boating is advertised on the River Derwent (near right).

◀ **MATLOCK BATH**
Derwent Terrace 1892 31277

Notice the boat houses in the foreground, where visitors could enjoy a skull along the Derwent as they still do today.

▲ **MATLOCK BATH,** *High Tor 1892* 31288

This great, 300ft vertical wall of limestone formed by the Derwent as it cut its impressive gorge between Matlock and Matlock Bath is known as High Tor. There have been 'recreation grounds' on the summit of the Tor for many years, and the view from the top is extensive. Today, the sheer face attracts rock climbers - it contains some of the most severe routes in the Peak District.

◄ **MATLOCK BATH**
The Heights of Abraham c1955 M47025

We are looking towards the Petrifying Well (centre right) in the centre of Matlock Bath. The well and fountain has been used for years to petrify objects placed in it, which are eventually coated with tufa from the lime-rich spring water. In the background, the wooded slopes lead up to Prospect Tower on the Heights of Abraham.

► MATLOCK BATH
North Parade 2002 M47701

Every summer weekend, Matlock Bath's North and South Parades become a bikers' paradise as motorcyclists from all over the East Midlands congregate to enjoy the scenery and admire each other's machines. This recent photograph shows the line-up of gleaming bikes on North Parade.

▼ MATLOCK BATH
From Temple Walk c1955
M47040

The Prospect Tower on the Heights of Abraham, which were named after General Wolfe's famous victory against the French at Quebec in 1759, can clearly be seen breaking through the trees on the left of this photograph. It is now the destination of the famous cable car ride across the Derwent Valley.

► TWO DALES
General View c1960
T206011

The steep Chesterfield Road winds up out of Two Dales, heading up Sydnope Hill for the heights of Matlock and Upper Moor. The edge of the moor can just be seen in the background.

◀ **WIRKSWORTH**
Adam Bede Cottage c1960
W351010

This small cottage on the Derby Road at Wirksworth is thought to be the place where the Victorian novelist George Eliot (Mary Ann Evans) set part of her famous book 'Adam Bede'. It was then the thatched home of George Eliot's aunt, Elizabeth Evans. Wirksworth is known in the book as 'Snowfield.'

► WIRKSWORTH
The Church c1960 W351014

Standing in a close almost like a cathedral, St Mary's church dates mainly from the 13th and 14th centuries, but it was heavily restored in 1876. Among its many treasures is an intricately carved 7th-century Saxon coffin lid, featuring stories from the life of Christ. There is also a famous little carving of a medieval lead miner – 't'owd man' – exemplifying the source of the town's wealth in the past.

▼ WIRKSWORTH
General View c1960 W351026

This long view across the quarrying town of Wirksworth was taken on a sunny day. Wirksworth is today the home of the National Stone Centre, which tells the fascinating story of the uses to which we put rocks won from quarries like those around the town. Appropriately, the centre is based in an abandoned quarry to the north of the town.

SOUTH CENTRAL

ASHFORD-IN-THE-WATER
From the Sheepwash Bridge c1955 A324018

The ancient Sheepwash Bridge was still in use by road traffic when this photograph was taken. It carried traffic into the village over the River Wye past the circular shelter just beyond the bridge. Today the bridge is used only by pedestrians.

ASHFORD-IN-THE-WATER
The Sheepwash Bridge c1965 A324032

Another view of the Sheepwash Bridge, this time from downstream and showing the walled enclosures which were used to direct sheep into the river so that their fleeces could be cleaned prior to shearing. Demonstrations of this ancient custom are still occasionally carried out by local farmers.

BAKEWELL, *From Castle Hill 1914* 67613A

Bakewell is the largest town in the Peak District National Park. Prominent is the spire of All Saints parish church; it stands on its hilltop site on the other side of the River Wye, which we can see below the spire.

BAKEWELL
South Church Street c1955 B6008

The spire and west end of the parish church rise above some old cottages. The church shows signs of a Saxon foundation, with many carved stones and two wayside crosses in the churchyard, but much of what we see today was the result of a severe 19th-century restoration.

BAKEWELL, *The Bridge c1955* B6006

Bakewell's fine five-arched Town Bridge over the River Wye dates from the 14th century, and is one of the oldest in the country still carrying traffic. Little has changed today from when this picture was taken, although there is new housing development beyond the trees on the left.

RUTLAND HOTEL

BAKEWELL
Rutland Square 1923
73888

The war memorial in the heart of Rutland Square is today surrounded by more extensive flowerbeds, but otherwise this scene is easily recognisable today. The Rutland Arms Hotel, where the Bakewell pudding was invented, still stands overlooking the square, with the parish church of All Saints on the hill behind.

► **BAKEWELL**
Rutland Square c1955 B6003

It is thirty years after No 73888, and little has changed here, where the A6 Derby Road joins the Chesterfield and Baslow Road in the centre of town. The trees of Bath Gardens can just be seen on the extreme right.

◄ **BAKEWELL**
Rutland Square c1955
B6022

We are looking from the upper windows of the Rutland Arms Hotel towards the Red Lion public house, the National Westminster Bank and the Old Pudding Shop in the centre of the picture. Burgon's grocery store on the right is now long gone, although older residents still refer to this as 'Burgon's Corner'. A faithful Hulley's bus from Baslow awaits passengers by the bus stop on the left.

▲ **CHATSWORTH HOUSE,** *1886* 18643

This is the classic view of the Duke of Devonshire's mainly 17th-century Derbyshire home, seen from James Paine's entrance bridge over the River Derwent. The only change that modern visitors to Derbyshire's most popular stately home will note are that the classical statues on the bridge piers are no longer present.

◄ **CHATSWORTH**
The Palm House c1876
8849

This very rare photograph, although titled The Palm House, shows what was usually known as the Great Conservatory, which was demolished in 1920. This magnificent 277ft (84m) by 123ft (38m) structure was the brainchild of Joseph Paxton, and at the time of its completion in 1840, it was the largest conservatory in the world. Using the experience he gained at Chatsworth, Paxton went on to design the Crystal Palace for the Great Exhibition in London in 1851.

EYAM
The Bull Ring 1919
69207

This view takes us back to another age. A pony and trap trots through the street as a crowd gathers in the background around a steam-powered traction engine. The Bull Ring took its name from the fact that bull-baiting once took place here, and the ring which held the bull is still visible in a corner of the square.

EYAM, *The Village Institute 1919* 69208X

The colonnaded building on the right of this photograph is the Village Institute, a kind of working men's club originally catering for the many lead miners who lived in the village. It stands opposite the trees of the churchyard in 37814 found on page 45.

EYAM
The Church 1896
37814

Eyam's parish church of St Lawrence has many memories of the tragic visitation of the plague in 1665-66. The heavily-restored church dates from the 13th century, and inside is a book showing the names of all the 350 victims of the plague, and the chair used by the rector, William Mompesson.

EYAM, *Eyam Hall 1896* 37816

Eyam Hall, dating from the late 17th century, has been in the hands of the Wright family for over 300 years. Recently opened to the public for the first time, it gives a wonderfully intimate view of a small country house, and has some fine tapestries in the upstairs rooms.

HADDON HALL
From the North-East c1870 5231

This is a seldom seen and unusual view of Haddon Hall, showing the Eagle Tower and the original entrance to the Upper Courtyard. The Eagle Tower dates from the 14th century and was built by Richard de Vernon.

◀ **HADDON HALL** *c1870* 5229

The romantic grey walls of Haddon Hall watch over the valley of the River Wye in this photograph, which was taken from Haddon Fields on the east bank of the river. Often described as the most perfect medieval manor house in England, Haddon Hall has been the Derbyshire home of the Dukes of Rutland for many generations.

▲ **MONYASH,** *Rake End c1960* M222010

The name 'Rake End' gives away the village's former dependence on lead mining, for 'rake' is the name given to a lead vein as it runs across country. Monyash, high on the White Peak plateau, formerly had its own lead mining or Barmote Court.

◀ **MONYASH** *Chapel Street c1960* M222016

It is easy to see how Chapel Street got its name – the mock-Gothic Methodist chapel stands on the right of this photograph. On the left of the picture, beyond the railings, lay Jack Mere, one of several village ponds or meres, which were so valuable on the fast-draining limestone plateau.

▼ **MONYASH,** *The Village Green c1960* M222020

We can just see the medieval village cross under the trees on the right. On the left is the Bull's Head public house, which recently reverted to its ancient name after an unfortunate experiment in calling it the Hobbit. The village blacksmith's shop was in the single storey building on the extreme left.

► **OVER HADDON**
Conksbury Bridge c1960 O77003

Conksbury Bridge, on the back road from Bakewell, is low-arched and narrow, and thought to be of medieval origin.

◄ **STONEY MIDDLETON**
Lover's Leap 1896
37820

This sleepy scene of the main valley road running through Stoney Middleton is vastly different today, as the main A623 Chesterfield to Chapel-en-le-Frith road is now heavy with traffic. The Lover's Leap of the title refers to the exploit of Hannah Baddeley, who threw herself from the limestone crag in the centre of the picture after she was jilted by her lover, but her voluminous skirts saved her.

► **STONEY MIDDLETON**
Looking East 1896
37823

This view shows Middleton Dale below the village, with the crags now so popular with rock climbers rising on the left, and the waste left by the old lime-burners in the foreground. Most of these workings are now invisible under the extensive tree growth which has burgeoned in the last century.

TADDINGTON
St Michael's Church c1960 T202001

St Michael's parish church, standing at over 1,000ft (300m) above the sea between Bakewell and Buxton, dates from the 12th century, but it was largely rebuilt during the 14th century. It features a rare stone lectern and a stone font dating from the 13th century.

TADDINGTON, *The Village c1960* T202005

The main street in Taddington used to be the main road between Bakewell and Buxton, but the village was one of the first in the country to be by-passed just after the Second World War. A single Morris car passes through, with the village chapel on the right.

TADDINGTON
The Dale c1960
T202007

This is the view from Humphrey Gate, above the one-street village of Taddington, which can be seen in the mid distance. Note the long, sunlit parallel lines of the dry stone walls reaching back from the village houses, which echo the areas of the strip fields of medieval times.

WINSTER, *From Rock Field c1955* W569005

The village of Winster lies near Bakewell. The name 'Rock Field' probably refers to former quarrying activities in the area. Much surface rock was cleared in the creation of the dry stone walls, such as the one running across the bottom of the picture.

YOULGRAVE
POST OFFICE

YOULGREAVE
Church Street c1955
Y14001

The splendid Perpendicular tower of All Saints' is one of the finest in the Peak District, and commands this view down Church Street. Note the charming Kate Greenaway-type silhouette sign above the village post office on the left, which uses the locally-preferred spelling of the village name: 'Youlgrave'.

CENTRAL REGION

BRADWELL
From Bradwell Edge c1955 B486025

This view shows the prominent chimney of the Hope Valley Cement Works at Hope (centre), a valuable source of employment for local people. Note the narrow walled fields leading off from the village street, which echo medieval strip cultivation. In the background is the Lose Hill/Back Tor ridge.

BRADWELL, *St Ives c1955* B486016

This part of Bradwell, where the Bradwell Brook is crossed by a narrow bridge, is known as St Ives, presumably because of its resemblance to the tight streets of the Cornish village. Note the old-fashioned red telephone box just over the bridge, and the cottages spreading up the hillside behind.

BRADWELL
The View from Smalldale c1955
B486046

Smalldale is the highest part of the village of Bradwell, and this view looks east down the steep hill and across the broad Hope Valley which spreads out into the distance.

CASTLETON, *View from the Castle 1919* 69166a

This view from the castle across the planned medieval township of Castleton at the head of the Hope Valley shows the parish church of St Edmund in the centre and Lose Hill across the valley in the left background. Castleton is unique among Peak District villages in that it is still mainly contained within a town ditch.

CASTLETON, *Peak Cavern 1919* 69172

These cottages at Goosehill stand on the lane which leads up to the entrance of Peak Cavern, whose entrance gapes under the limestone crags visible in the background. The stream which issues from the cave entrance is Peakshole Water.

▼ **CASTLETON,** *Peak Cavern 1896* 37847

Peak Cavern has the largest entrance to any cave system in Britain, and was used for generations of rope-makers - their equipment can be seen here. The cavern owners recently controversially changed its name to its ancient one of 'The Devil's Arse'.

► **CASTLETON**
Peveril Castle 1896
37838

A close-up view of Henry I's 12th-century keep at Peveril Castle, overlooking Castleton. It was at Peveril that Henry accepted the submission of King Malcolm of Scotland in 1157, and he built this splendid, stone-built keep 19 years later. It remains the finest medieval landmark in the Peak, and was formerly the symbol of the Peak District National Park.

CASTLETON
Bargate 1932
85233

Bargate, or Siggate, leads down to the Market Place, which is surrounded by fine 17th- and 18th-century buildings. The entrance to Cave Dale leads off to the left, in front of the whitewashed cottage. In the background are the distant outlines of Treak Cliff and Mam Tor.

CASTLETON
Winnats Pass 1932
85240

The entrance to Castleton from the west is through the impressive limestone gorge known as The Winnats – a corruption of 'wind gates'. This view shows a single-track lane winding through the gorge, with a white weighing machine standing outside the entrance to Speedwell Cavern on the left. Since the collapse of the Mam Tor road in the 1970s, the Winnats is now once again the main route into Castleton from the west.

CASTLETON
The Boat at Halfway House, Speedwell Cavern c1960 C46082

Speedwell Cavern at the foot of the Winnats Pass is unique among the Castleton show caves because it is reached by a half-mile boat trip. Here, the boat arrives at the Halfway House on its way to its destination - the Bottomless Pit. The cavern was discovered by lead miners, who had cut the underground canal to drain their mine of excess water.

CHEE DALE
1914 67601

The River Wye rushes spectacularly through the confines of Chee Dale, to the west of Bakewell, as the limestone cliffs crowd in. Extensive stands of butterbur, so-called because its large, rhubarb-like leaves were once used to wrap butter to keep it fresh, can be seen on the left of the photograph.

CHEE DALE
1996 C72701

The Midland Line was constructed through the Wye Valley and Chee Dale in 1863, exciting the wrath of early conservationists like John Ruskin. This modern view of Chee Dale, with Plum Buttress on the right, shows one of many viaducts which had to be constructed on the left. The line is known today as the Monsal Trail, and is used by walkers and riders. There are long-term plans to restore trains to the line (see also No M221005).

▲ **CHELMORTON,** *The Village c1960* C401009

Chelmorton, high on the limestone plateau to the east of Buxton, is one of the highest villages in Derbyshire, standing at over 1,000ft (300m) above the sea. This photograph shows the centre of the one-street village. Note the school sign in the centre of the photograph.

◄ **GREAT HUCKLOW**
The Florence Nightingale War Memorial Home c1950
G180002

This Home took the name of one of Derbyshire's greatest heroines. Florence Nightingale, who bravely nursed the victims of the Crimean War, hailed from Holloway, near Matlock.

HATHERSAGE
The Village 1902 48915

We are looking towards the George Hotel, a former coaching inn, in the centre of the photograph. Houses and shops now fill the foreground of the picture, and the stream in the foreground has been culverted.

HATHERSAGE
The Villas 1902 48916

These are typical early 20th-century villas, built perhaps for the first commuters to nearby Sheffield, in Station Road. Note the then-fashionable bay windows and half-tiled frontages.

◄ **HATHERSAGE**
General View
1919 69190

This is the eastern approach from the Surprise View road into the Hope Valley village of Hathersage. Note the steam rising from a train just approaching the Totley tunnel on the Hope Valley line on the extreme left.

▲ **HATHERSAGE,** *The Church 1932* 85252

The hilltop parish church of St Michael has watched over the village for more than 900 years, but much of the present building dates from the 14th and 15th centuries. It is famous for its wonderful brasses commemorating the Eyres, a prominent local family on whom Charlotte Bronte based characters in her novel 'Jane Eyre'.

◄ **HATHERSAGE**
Little John's Grave
1902 48920

The other thing that Hathersage churchyard is famous for is this 10ft-long grave between two venerable yew trees (now severely pruned) which is said to be the last resting place of Robin Hood's faithful lieutenant, Little John. Whether the 'John Little', a nailor of Hathersage, was really Little John, or whether Robin Hood ever existed, is still a matter for debate.

HATHERSAGE
Brookfield Manor 1902 48932

Brookfield Manor is a stately Victorian house built in the valley of the Hood Brook (another Robin Hood connection?) to the north of Hathersage. Later a training centre for British Steel from nearby Sheffield, the house is now run as a conference centre.

HATHERSAGE, *The River Derwent 1919* 69197

This view was taken from the Leadmill Bridge at Hathersage. On the skyline we can see the crags of Millstone Edge, now popular with rock climbers. But this face is artificial, created by quarrymen who were engaged in one of Hathersage's traditional industries, the making of mill and grind stones.

HATHERSAGE
The Road to Grindleford 1919
69205

The slopes to the left are now largely covered by trees, but the Grindleford road from Hathersage still winds along the valley of the River Derwent, which is hidden on the right. Note the hay bales in the field in the right middle distance.

HATHERSAGE, *Toad's Mouth Rock c1963* H38033

Someone once carved an eye on this strangely-shaped gritstone boulder to increase its resemblance to the warty amphibian and give it its name. Toad's Mouth stands on the moors to the east of Hathersage near Burbage Bridge, where it overhangs the A625 Fox House road.

HOPE
The Old Hall Hotel 1919 69180

This view of the centre of the village shows the Old Hall Hotel in the centre background, with an early motor car parked outside. Two lads chat outside the old village smithy, on the extreme right foreground, and the raised, walled churchyard is on the left. The Old Hall Hotel retains the name today; it stands on the site of the medieval Old Hall of the Balguy family.

HOPE
1919 69179

The village of Hope gave its name to the long east-west valley which ends at Castleton. The squat spire of Hope's 14th-century parish church of St Peter dominates the village, with the slopes of Win Hill in the background to the right.

HOPE, *St Peter's Church, the South Door 1932* 85263

The churchyard at Hope is filled with gravestones commemorating local families, such as the Eyres and the Woodruffes. But its most important feature is the shaft of a Saxon preaching cross (just visible at the far end of the church), which is thought to date from the 9th century.

HOPE, *The Church c1955* H113026

We are looking at the eastern end of St Peter's parish church from the main road. The church dates from Saxon and Norman times, when the village was an important centre of the Royal Forest of the Peak, a hunting preserve of Norman monarchs.

▼ **HOPE,** *Moorgate and Lose Hill 1920* 69184

Lose Hill, at 1,563ft (476m) is the eastern extremity of a fine ridge which runs from Mam Tor. It overlooks the village of Hope and the white-gabled house known as Moorgate (centre right), which now serves as a Countrywide (formerly Co-operative) Holidays Association guest house.

► **LITTON MILL**
The Village c1955
L561004

These cottages at Litton Mill were built to house employees at the local cotton mill, which gave the hamlet its name. Some of the worst atrocities of child labour were allegedly perpetrated at the mill during the 19th century. These cottages are now, like so many in the Peak District, often taken over as holiday homes for visitors to the National Park.

MILLER'S DALE
The Village 1914
67598

This tiny hamlet was put on the map in the 1860s by the Midland Railway – Miller's Dale was the junction for the spa town of Buxton. The River Wye passes through a deep gorge here, beneath the Victorian Gothic parish church of St Anne, built in 1880 by Canon Samuel Andrew of nearby Tideswell.

MONSAL DALE
From the Bridge c1864 2146

This clapper-style footbridge in Upperdale, Monsal Dale could be very ancient indeed, as this is one of the most primitive of bridge-building styles. It is more likely, however, that it has been swept away by the floodwaters of the Wye many times, and that this was a relatively modern replacement.

◄**MONSAL DALE**
The Monsal Head Hotel c1955 M221004

The wooden balcony of the Monsal Head Hotel gives the building a strangely Tyrolean effect, quite out of place in the Peak District. The hotel has one of the finest views in the Derbyshire dales (see M221005 above).

◀ **MONSAL DALE**
The Viaduct c1955 M221005

A south-bound steam train thunders across the Monsal Head viaduct. This stately five-arched structure now carries the Monsal Trail; and despite John Ruskin's outburst when it was being built, it is now a protected structure. In the background on the left are the slopes of Fin Cop, which is topped by an Iron Age hill fort.

▲ **PEAK DALE,** *Small Dale c1955* P235004

Farm buildings and cottages in the hamlet of Small Dale, north of Peak Dale, to the north-east of Buxton. This whole area is now blighted by huge limestone quarries, including the one at Tunstead, which has one of the longest quarry faces in Europe.

◀ **PEAK DALE**
c1955 P235005

Evidence of that quarrying activity is provided by this photograph of Peak Dale, taken looking towards the quarry faces at Tunstead. The huge conical spoil tip in the centre of the photograph is long gone, as quarrying companies now have to pay much more regard to the landscape of Britain's first National Park.

▼ **PEAK DALE,** *Holy Trinity Church c1960* P235009

The Victorian parish church of the Holy Trinity is simple, whitewashed and towerless. Many of Peak Dale's residents worked at the nearby limestone quarries, continuing the traditional dual economies of farming and mining which had long been the mainstay of local communities.

► **TIDESWELL**
The Church c1960
T46018

Tideswell's parish church of St John the Baptist is known as 'the Cathedral of the Peak' for very good reason. The Decorated church was built in the relatively short period of between 1300-1370, and shows a pleasing uniformity not usually found in such buildings.

TIDESWELL
Well Dressing 2000 T46701

The age-old Peak District custom of 'dressing' village wells or springs to give thanks for water is undertaken annually at Tideswell in on the Saturday nearest the patronal festival of St John the Baptist on 24 June. This modern photograph shows the Town Well being admired by a group of visitors.

TIDESWELL
The Parish Church, the Chancel c1960
T46019

The great glory of Tideswell's parish church is the chancel, where the clear medieval glass of the large windows gives it a wonderfully light and airy atmosphere. In the right foreground we can see some of the work of the famous Hunstone family of wood-carvers from the village.

THE EAST

BAMFORD

The Church 1919 69176

Bamford's parish church of St John the Baptist was largely restored by William Butterfield in 1861. It is probably most famous for the fact that the dead from the drowned village of Derwent were re-interred in its churchyard after the construction of the Ladybower Dam during the Second World War.

BAMFORD
The Marquis of Granby Hotel c1955
B483031

The imposing Marquis of Granby is a landmark on the main Hope Valley road, near the turn (now with traffic lights) to Bamford and Derwent. Named after a prominent local landlord, the Marquis is currently empty and awaiting a new use. The long ridge of Shatton Edge rises in the background.

BAMFORD, *The Derwent Valley Reservoir and Howden Dam c1965* B483039

This fine view of the overflowing Howden Dam, with the forbidding moorlands of Bleaklow beyond, is taken from Abbey Bank on edge of the Howden Moors. The Howden Dam was built between 1901 and 1912, and was the first in the series of three in the Derwent Valley to be completed.

BASLOW
The Bridge c1870 5217

Beeches frame Baslow's three-arched medieval bridge at Nether End, as it strides the River Derwent with elegant ease. It is one of two bridges in the village – the other one at Bridge End dates from the 17th century and features a tiny toll-house with a 3½ ft (1m) high doorway. Note the thatched cottages on the left – a rarity in the Peak District.

BASLOW
The Village c1955
B484006

On the right in this view of the Derwentside village of Baslow is the lych gate to the parish church of St Anne, which has an unusual clock face bearing the legend VICTORIA 1897 instead of numbers, in celebration of the Queen's jubilee that year. Opposite the church is Coates' former grocery and chemist's shop.

▲ **CALVER,** *The Village c1950* C399045

This crossroads west of the village of Calver is known as Calver Sough – a sough (pronounced 'suff') is a drainage tunnel to take water out of lead mines. There are traffic lights here today at the busy junction of the Bakewell-Grindleford and Baslow-Stoney Middleton roads, and the petrol station on the right is now a shop selling outdoor equipment.

◀ **CALVER**
Curbar Edge c1950
C399082

This photograph was taken from the Bakewell road outside Calver. The pronounced nick on the skyline is Curbar Gap, where a road winds up from the Derwent Valley to cross the moors towards Sheffield. Note the caravans parked haphazardly in the fields below, as the first signs of mass tourism impinge on the scene.

▼ FROGGATT, *The Bridge 1896* 37807

This elegant double-span bridge over the River Derwent dates from the 17th century, and is unusual in that it has a large, pointed central arch nearer to the village and a smaller one on the other side. The smaller arch probably formed part of the original, smaller structure.

► GRINDLEFORD
The Bridge 1896 37806

This fine, three-arched bridge takes the main village street of Grindleford over the River Derwent and up towards the moors to the east. It is now controlled by traffic lights, but when this photograph was taken, there was no need for such restrictions.

◄ **GRINDLEFORD**
The War Memorial c1960 G182003

The war memorial at the foot of Sir William Hill is based on Eyam's truncated Saxon cross, and stands on what was once the village green and the centre of the village. It is now on the Hathersage road out of the village, which spreads in linear fashion along the banks of the River Derwent.

► **GRINDLEFORD**
Upper Padley c1960 G182010

This leafy lane leads from Grindleford to the woods of Padley Gorge, now in the care of the National Trust. Upper Padley is well known for the Catholic shrine of Padley Chapel, in what remains of the gatehouse of Padley Hall. Here, two recusant Catholic priests were arrested in 1588 and were later hanged, drawn and quartered by the authorities at Derby.

GRINDLEFORD
The View from Goatscliff c1960
G182020

The Goatscliff entrance to the village of Grindleford from Bakewell is little changed today. In the background are the wooded slopes of Froggatt and White Edge and the National Trust's Longshaw Estate.

GRINDLEFORD
The Village c1960
G182028

A mini van is parked outside the Derwent Stores in the main street. Perhaps a sign of the times, the shop is now an art gallery, and the village stores is now down the road near the bridge over the River Derwent.

LADYBOWER, *The Reservoir c1955* L294003

A lone car speeds across the Ashopton viaduct of the Ladybower Reservoir. Under the arches of this massive structure are what remains of the village of Ashopton, which was depopulated and demolished when the reservoir was constructed between 1943 and 1953.

LADYBOWER
The Dam and Win Hill c1955 L294006

This view looks across the ornate, wrought iron gates of the Ladybower Dam towards the newly planted regimented forestry plantations on the slopes of Win Hill. The Ladybower Dam was opened by King George VI at these gates on 25 September 1945.

LADYBOWER, *The Reservoir and Derwent Dam c1955* L294012

This is an interesting view of the northern end of the Ladybower Reservoir, taken at a time of low water. It shows the castellated towers of the Derwent Dam in the background, and the remains of a farmhouse on the left, which could be Fairholmes Farm, after which the modern visitor centre near here takes its name.

▼ **ROWSLEY,** *The Peacock Inn c1864* 2151

The mellow ivy-covered gritstone walls of the Peacock Hotel on the A6 about four miles north of Matlock are a landmark for visitors coming into the Peak District from the south. The inn dates from the mid 17th century; it was originally a manor house for the agent to the Manners family at nearby Haddon Hall, whose peacock crest we can see over the porch.

► **STOCKSBRIDGE**
Langsett Reservoir c1955 S324024

Langsett Reservoir was constructed between 1889 and 1904 by an army of navvies. They lived in a temporary village, which included a hospital, a canteen and recreation rooms, beneath the dam wall on the right. The castellated valvehouse which we can just see at the far end of the embankment was modelled on the gatehouse of Lancaster Castle.

◄ **STOCKSBRIDGE**
The Ewden Valley c1955 S324011

This pastoral view of the Ewden Valley to the west of Sheffield shows the Broomhead Reservoir, one of a series constructed in the late 19th and early 20th centuries to supply the needs of the neighbouring fast-expanding industrial city of Sheffield.

► **STOCKSBRIDGE**
Underbank Reservoir c1955
S324029

Underbank Reservoir in the valley of the River Don just above Stocksbridge is yet another of the more than 50 reservoirs which flood the steep-sided valleys of the Dark Peak. Their proximity to the great cities made them very convenient for the water engineers of the late 19th and early 20th centuries.

THE WEST

BUXTON
The Crescent c1862 1457

Buxton's greatest architectural glory is the elegant, sweeping curve of John Carr's Crescent, built in 1784 by the 5th Duke of Devonshire as he tried to make Buxton a spa to rival Bath. It was still St Ann's Hotel when this photograph was taken, but more recently it fell into disuse; it has now been restored by English Heritage after years of neglect. In the background we can see the newly-built Palace Hotel.

BUXTON
Spring Gardens
1923 74121

We are viewing the end of the Crescent Hotel and the Thermal Baths from Spring Gardens. Buxton's warm springs are thought to have been first discovered by the Romans, but it was the Duke of Devonshire who really popularised the lofty Georgian town (it stands at over 1,000ft above the sea), with developments like the Thermal Baths.

BUXTON
Cavendish Arcade
2000 B263702

This view from The Quadrant, almost the same spot as No 74121 but 80 years later, shows the Thermal Baths, now labelled Buxton Baths and housing the Cavendish Arcade shopping centre. The lamp-topped memorial in the centre of both photographs is to Samuel Turner, a churchwarden at St John's church for over 30 years, a trustee of the Devonshire Hospital, and a prominent local builder.

▲ **BUXTON,** *The Pavilion 2000* B263701

Buxton's Pavilion in Pavilion Gardens was designed and built by Edward Milner of Sydenham in 1871 to allow visitors who were taking the waters the space to take exercise indoors, away from Buxton's notoriously cold weather. This modern view shows the exterior and dome to the left.

◄ **BUXTON**
The Pavilion, the Interior 1890 24734

This interior shot of the Pavilion shows the beautiful cast iron tracery, the sumptuous curtaining and the exotic potted plants which decorated the exercise area. On the right a couple, partly obscured, sit among the plants enjoying the warm, humid air of the Pavilion.

BUXTON
Pavilion Gardens
c1871 5201

The Serpentine Walks in Buxton's Pavilion Gardens were carefully landscaped by Milner to give visitors to the spa a pleasant, relaxing experience after their treatment. Over a century later, the Pavilion Gardens still provide the nucleus of the town's leisure activities, with Frank Matcham's beautifully-restored Opera House close by.

BUXTON

The Railway Bridge over the River Wye c1870 5215

A solitary pony and trap pass under the Midland Railway bridge at Topley Pike, on what is now the A6 on the outskirts of Buxton. The railway was newly-built when this photograph was taken, as we can see from the gleaming steelwork of the bridge. The limestone crag of Topley Pike rises in the background.

BUXTON, *Poole's Cavern Gardens c1862* 1461

Poole's Cavern has been a major tourist attraction ever since Mary Queen of Scots visited it during her incarceration at the Old Hall in the 16th century. Three centuries later, its landscaped gardens were studded with niches for classical statuary and urns.

CAT AND FIDDLE
JOSEPH TOMLINSON.

BUXTON
The Cat and Fiddle Inn 1914 67581A

A wonderful array of early motor cars, plus a motorcycle with a wickerwork sidecar on the right. The Cat and Fiddle on the moors above Buxton is the second-highest public house in England, standing at 1,690ft/515m above the sea, and is a welcome landmark on the lonely Buxton-Macclesfield road.

▲ **LEEK**
Derby Street c1960 L379002

This early traffic roundabout is situated at the junction of the A53 Buxton to Stoke-on-Trent road with the A523 Macclesfield road. It is interesting to note the lack of any sign of traffic, a telling reminder of a bygone, slower-paced age.

► **LEEK**
The Monument c1960 L379005

The grand white marble clock tower of the Nicholson War Memorial dominates this view of Leek town centre. It might be more correctly known as a peace memorial; it was raised by local worthy Sir Arthur Nicholson in memory of his own son and all the other sons of Leek who died during the First World War.

LEEK, *St Edward's Church c1960* L379008

St Edward the Confessor, the mother church of the Staffordshire moorland town of Leek, is a fine building, with a pinnacled 14th-century tower. Its churchyard has the unusual distinction of recording a double sunset at the summer solstice, when the sun seems to set twice as it drops below the distant hill known as The Cloud.

▼ **LEEK,** *The Roaches c1960* L379020

A distant view from the A53 Buxton road of the dramatic outline of Hen Cloud, on the right, and the Roaches on the left, just outside Leek. Both these gritstone outcrops provide wonderful views across the Cheshire Plain, and great routes of all standards for rock climbers.

► **RAINOW**
General View c1955
R307005

This view from the edge of the village shows the rolling nature of the landscape where the westernmost hills of the Peak District drop down towards the fertile flatlands of the Cheshire Plain.

◀ **RAINOW**
General View c1955 R307007

This hillside village stands on the western side of the Peak District in Cheshire. The Perpendicular tower of the parish church watches over the scattered houses. Rainow stands where the A537 Buxton-Macclesfield moorland road descends towards the Cheshire Plain.

▶ **WILDBOARCLOUGH**
St Saviour's Parish Church c1960
W369002

The squat sandstone building of St Saviour's parish church is surrounded by rhododendrons in this secluded valley on the western edge of the Peak District. Said to be the last place in England where a wild boar was killed, Wildboarclough shelters under the shapely cone of Shutlingsloe, one of the only true 'peaks' in the Peak District.

WILDBOARCLOUGH
The Crag Inn c1960
W369010

We are looking from the banks of the Clough Brook. The Crag Inn takes its name from the old name of the village. It is still a popular eating and drinking place, hidden away among the hills in this secret valley in the Cheshire Pennines.

WILDBOARCLOUGH, *Crag Hall and Shutlingsloe c1960* W369012

The gable-like ridge of Shutlingsloe, whose summit is 1,659ft/506m above the sea, dominates almost every view of Wildboarclough, such as this one from Crag Hall. It commands tremendous views west across Manchester and the Cheshire Plain and eastwards into the Peak District hills.

THE NORTH

CHAPEL-EN-LE-FRITH
Chinley from Eccles Pike c1960 C400027

Seen from the 1,214ft/370m summit of Eccles Pike, the village of Chinley occupies the bottom of the valley of the Black Brook, with Cracken Edge and the Naze beyond. Chinley really took off with the coming of the railway in 1902, which was carried by two magnificent curving viaducts which take the line across the valley.

▶ **EDALE**
Composite Postcard c1960
E129061

This composite postcard shows the winding route of the Pennine Way north from Edale, up the highest ground in the Pennines to the Scottish border. The other pictures show (top to bottom) the River Noe, which runs through the Edale Valley, and Lose Hill; Mam Tor at Castleton; and Edale's Nag's Head Inn.

▼ **CHAPEL-EN-LE-FRITH**
The Cross c1960 C400034

The old market cross in Chapel en le Frith's Market Place is undated, but it is almost certainly medieval in origin. Chapel was established between 1220 and 1230 as a borough entitled to hold markets and fairs, and the original parish church was built around 1225.

▶ **EDALE**
The Nag's Head Hotel c1955
E129002

The Old Nag's Head Hotel is perhaps best known as the starting point for the Pennine Way, Britain's first and toughest National Trail, which wends for 270 miles up England's backbone to the Scottish border. The inn was built in 1577, probably to serve the packhorse teams which used the tiny bridge across the Grinds Brook below it, having crossed the peaty wastes of Kinder Scout. In the background we can see the headland of the Nab.

◀ **EDALE**
The Parish Church c1955
E129014

The parish church of the Holy Trinity was built in 1885 to replace a chapel of ease for Castleton's church which had been built in 1633 and was sited across the road in the old churchyard. Before Edale's church and chapel were built, worshippers had to walk three miles and climb 600ft/183m to attend services at Castleton.

HAYFIELD
Market Street c1960
H298002

A couple of lads chat outside the bank on the corner of Market Street. This sleepy little Pennine town on the western slopes of Kinder Scout formerly had wool, cotton, papermaking and textile printing mills, all powered by the fast-flowing waters of the Kinder and Sett Rivers.

▲ **HOLMFIRTH**
The Holme Valley from Holme Moss c1955 H212015

Two rather grubby-looking sheep graze on the lower slopes of Holme Moss, with Brownhills Reservoir and the town of Holmfirth in the right background. The ridgetop village of Holme occupies the centre of the photograph.

► **HOLMFIRTH**
Holme Moss Television Mast c1955 H212021

The 740ft/225m-high needle-like mast on the summit of 1,718ft/524m Holme Moss started transmitting television pictures to 16 million homes in a large area of northern England in 1951. Weather conditions on this exposed Pennine hilltop can be severe, and in the winter of 1986, a block of ice weighing two tons which had formed on the mast crashed through the roof of the transmission station beneath.

▲ **TINTWISTLE**
The Village Centre c1960 T204028

Tintwistle – locally pronounced 'Tinsel' – stands at the entrance to Longdendale in the far north-west of the Peak District. This view shows typical Pennine gritstone terraces lining the street, which leads into the wilds of the Longdendale-Woodhead cross-Pennine route.

◄ **TINTWISTLE**
The Parish Church c1960 T204008

The Victorian parish church of Christ the King dominates this view of the village, seen from across the bridge crossing the River Etherow in the foreground. Tintwistle Low Moor is in the background.

TINTWISTLE
The Longdendale Valley c1960 T204024

This view from the Woodhead Road across Valehouse Reservoir towards the distant slopes of Peaknaze Moor and Bramah Edge on Bleaklow shows how the valley has been changed by man. At the time they were built, between 1848 and 1862, the string of five reservoirs which filled the bottom of the valley constituted the largest stretch of man-made water in the world.

WHALEY BRIDGE, *Toddbrook Reservoir c1955* W346007

Toddbrook Reservoir, south of Whaley Bridge, dams the Todd Brook just before it reaches the River Goyt. This view looks across the reservoir towards Slatersbank Wood and the distant slopes of Chinley Churn. Today the reservoir is the site of a thriving sailing club.

INDEX

Frith Book Co Titles

www.francisfrith.co.uk

The Frith Book Company publishes over 100 new titles each year. A selection of those currently available is listed below. For latest catalogue please contact Frith Book Co.

Town Books 96 pages, approximately 100 photos. ***County and Themed Books*** 128 pages, approximately 150 photos (unless specified). All titles hardback with laminated case and jacket, except those indicated pb (paperback)

Amersham, Chesham & Rickmansworth (pb)	1-85937-340-2	£9.99
Andover (pb)	1-85937-292-9	£9.99
Aylesbury (pb)	1-85937-227-9	£9.99
Barnstaple (pb)	1-85937-300-3	£9.99
Basildon Living Memories (pb)	1-85937-515-4	£9.99
Bath (pb)	1-85937-419-0	£9.99
Bedford (pb)	1-85937-205-8	£9.99
Bedfordshire Living Memories	1-85937-513-8	£14.99
Belfast (pb)	1-85937-303-8	£9.99
Berkshire (pb)	1-85937-191-4	£9.99
Berkshire Churches	1-85937-170-1	£17.99
Berkshire Living Memories	1-85937-332-1	£14.99
Black Country	1-85937-497-2	£12.99
Blackpool (pb)	1-85937-393-3	£9.99
Bognor Regis (pb)	1-85937-431-x	£9.99
Bournemouth (pb)	1-85937-545-6	£9.99
Bradford (pb)	1-85937-204-x	£9.99
Bridgend (pb)	1-85937-386-0	£7.99
Bridgwater (pb)	1-85937-305-4	£9.99
Bridport (pb)	1-85937-327-5	£9.99
Brighton (pb)	1-85937-192-2	£8.99
Bristol (pb)	1-85937-264-3	£9.99
British Life A Century Ago (pb)	1-85937-213-9	£9.99
Buckinghamshire (pb)	1-85937-200-7	£9.99
Camberley (pb)	1-85937-222-8	£9.99
Cambridge (pb)	1-85937-422-0	£9.99
Cambridgeshire (pb)	1-85937-420-4	£9.99
Cambridgeshire Villages	1-85937-523-5	£14.99
Canals And Waterways (pb)	1-85937-291-0	£9.99
Canterbury Cathedral (pb)	1-85937-179-5	£9.99
Cardiff (pb)	1-85937-093-4	£9.99
Carmarthenshire (pb)	1-85937-604-5	£9.99
Chelmsford (pb)	1-85937-310-0	£9.99
Cheltenham (pb)	1-85937-095-0	£9.99
Cheshire (pb)	1-85937-271-6	£9.99
Chester (pb)	1-85937-382 8	£9.99
Chesterfield (pb)	1-85937-378-x	£9.99
Chichester (pb)	1-85937-228-7	£9.99
Churches of East Cornwall (pb)	1-85937-249-x	£9.99
Churches of Hampshire (pb)	1-85937-207-4	£9.99
Cinque Ports & Two Ancient Towns	1-85937-492-1	£14.99
Colchester (pb)	1-85937-188-4	£8.99
Cornwall (pb)	1-85937-229-5	£9.99
Cornwall Living Memories	1-85937-248-1	£14.99
Cotswolds (pb)	1-85937-230-9	£9.99
Cotswolds Living Memories	1-85937-255-4	£14.99
County Durham (pb)	1-85937-398-4	£9.99
Croydon Living Memories (pb)	1-85937-162-0	£9.99
Cumbria (pb)	1-85937-621-5	£9.99
Derby (pb)	1-85937-367-4	£9.99
Derbyshire (pb)	1-85937-196-5	£9.99
Derbyshire Living Memories	1-85937-330-5	£14.99
Devon (pb)	1-85937-297-x	£9.99
Devon Churches (pb)	1-85937-250-3	£9.99
Dorchester (pb)	1-85937-307-0	£9.99
Dorset (pb)	1-85937-269-4	£9.99
Dorset Coast (pb)	1-85937-299-6	£9.99
Dorset Living Memories (pb)	1-85937-584-7	£9.99
Down the Severn (pb)	1-85937-560-x	£9.99
Down The Thames (pb)	1-85937-278-3	£9.99
Down the Trent	1-85937-311-9	£14.99
East Anglia (pb)	1-85937-265-1	£9.99
East Grinstead (pb)	1-85937-138-8	£9.99
East London	1-85937-080-2	£14.99
East Sussex (pb)	1-85937-606-1	£9.99
Eastbourne (pb)	1-85937-399-2	£9.99
Edinburgh (pb)	1-85937-193-0	£8.99
England In The 1880s	1-85937-331-3	£17.99
Essex - Second Selection	1-85937-456-5	£14.99
Essex (pb)	1-85937-270-8	£9.99
Essex Coast	1-85937-342-9	£14.99
Essex Living Memories	1-85937-490-5	£14.99
Exeter	1-85937-539-1	£9.99
Exmoor (pb)	1-85937-608-8	£9.99
Falmouth (pb)	1-85937-594-4	£9.99
Folkestone (pb)	1-85937-124-8	£9.99
Frome (pb)	1-85937-317-8	£9.99
Glamorgan	1-85937-488-3	£14.99
Glasgow (pb)	1-85937-190-6	£9.99
Glastonbury (pb)	1-85937-338-0	£7.99
Gloucester (pb)	1-85937-232-5	£9.99
Gloucestershire (pb)	1-85937-561-8	£9.99
Great Yarmouth (pb)	1-85937-426-3	£9.99
Greater Manchester (pb)	1-85937-266-x	£9.99
Guildford (pb)	1-85937-410-7	£9.99
Hampshire (pb)	1-85937-279-1	£9.99
Harrogate (pb)	1-85937-423-9	£9.99
Hastings and Bexhill (pb)	1-85937-131-0	£9.99
Heart of Lancashire (pb)	1-85937-197-3	£9.99
Helston (pb)	1-85937-214-7	£9.99
Hereford (pb)	1-85937-175-2	£9.99
Herefordshire (pb)	1-85937-567-7	£9.99
Herefordshire Living Memories	1-85937-514-6	£14.99
Hertfordshire (pb)	1-85937-247-3	£9.99
Horsham (pb)	1-85937-432-8	£9.99
Humberside (pb)	1-85937-605-3	£9.99
Hythe, Romney Marsh, Ashford (pb)	1-85937-256-2	£9.99
Ipswich (pb)	1-85937-424-7	£9.99
Isle of Man (pb)	1-85937-268-6	£9.99
Isle of Wight (pb)	1-85937-429-8	£9.99
Isle of Wight Living Memories	1-85937-304-6	£14.99
Kent (pb)	1-85937-189-2	£9.99
Kent Living Memories(pb)	1-85937-401-8	£9.99
Kings Lynn (pb)	1-85937-334-8	£9.99

Available from your local bookshop or from the publisher

Frith Book Co Titles (continued)

Lake District (pb)	1-85937-275-9	£9.99
Lancashire Living Memories	1-85937-335-6	£14.99
Lancaster, Morecambe, Heysham (pb)	1-85937-233-3	£9.99
Leeds (pb)	1-85937-202-3	£9.99
Leicester (pb)	1-85937-381-x	£9.99
Leicestershire & Rutland Living Memories	1-85937-500-6	£12.99
Leicestershire (pb)	1-85937-185-x	£9.99
Lighthouses	1-85937-257-0	£9.99
Lincoln (pb)	1-85937-380-1	£9.99
Lincolnshire (pb)	1-85937-433-6	£9.99
Liverpool and Merseyside (pb)	1-85937-234-1	£9.99
London (pb)	1-85937-183-3	£9.99
London Living Memories	1-85937-454-9	£14.99
Ludlow (pb)	1-85937-176-0	£9.99
Luton (pb)	1-85937-235-x	£9.99
Maidenhead (pb)	1-85937-339-9	£9.99
Maidstone (pb)	1-85937-391-7	£9.99
Manchester (pb)	1-85937-198-1	£9.99
Marlborough (pb)	1-85937-336-4	£9.99
Middlesex	1-85937-158-2	£14.99
Monmouthshire	1-85937-532-4	£14.99
New Forest (pb)	1-85937-390-9	£9.99
Newark (pb)	1-85937-366-6	£9.99
Newport, Wales (pb)	1-85937-258-9	£9.99
Newquay (pb)	1-85937-421-2	£9.99
Norfolk (pb)	1-85937-195-7	£9.99
Norfolk Broads	1-85937-486-7	£14.99
Norfolk Living Memories (pb)	1-85937-402-6	£9.99
North Buckinghamshire	1-85937-626-6	£14.99
North Devon Living Memories	1-85937-261-9	£14.99
North Hertfordshire	1-85937-547-2	£14.99
North London (pb)	1-85937-403-4	£9.99
North Somerset	1-85937-302-x	£14.99
North Wales (pb)	1-85937-298-8	£9.99
North Yorkshire (pb)	1-85937-236-8	£9.99
Northamptonshire Living Memories	1-85937-529-4	£14.99
Northamptonshire	1-85937-150-7	£14.99
Northumberland Tyne & Wear (pb)	1-85937-281-3	£9.99
Northumberland	1-85937-522-7	£14.99
Norwich (pb)	1-85937-194-9	£8.99
Nottingham (pb)	1-85937-324-0	£9.99
Nottinghamshire (pb)	1-85937-187-6	£9.99
Oxford (pb)	1-85937-411-5	£9.99
Oxfordshire (pb)	1-85937-430-1	£9.99
Oxfordshire Living Memories	1-85937-525-1	£14.99
Paignton (pb)	1-85937-374-7	£7.99
Peak District (pb)	1-85937-280-5	£9.99
Pembrokeshire	1-85937-262-7	£14.99
Penzance (pb)	1-85937-595-2	£9.99
Peterborough (pb)	1-85937-219-8	£9.99
Picturesque Harbours	1-85937-208-2	£14.99
Piers	1-85937-237-6	£17.99
Plymouth (pb)	1-85937-389-5	£9.99
Poole & Sandbanks (pb)	1-85937-251-1	£9.99
Preston (pb)	1-85937-212-0	£9.99
Reading (pb)	1-85937-238-4	£9.99
Redhill to Reigate (pb)	1-85937-596-0	£9.99
Ringwood (pb)	1-85937-384-4	£7.99
Romford (pb)	1-85937-319-4	£9.99
Royal Tunbridge Wells (pb)	1-85937-504-9	£9.99
Salisbury (pb)	1-85937-239-2	£9.99
Scarborough (pb)	1-85937-379-8	£9.99
Sevenoaks and Tonbridge (pb)	1-85937-392-5	£9.99
Sheffield & South Yorks (pb)	1-85937-267-8	£9.99
Sherborne (pb)	1-85937-301-1	£9.99
Shrewsbury (pb)	1-85937-325-9	£9.99
Shropshire (pb)	1-85937-326-7	£9.99
Shropshire Living Memories	1-85937-643-6	£14.99
Somerset	1-85937-153-1	£14.99
South Devon Coast	1-85937-107-8	£14.99
South Devon Living Memories (pb)	1-85937-609-6	£9.99
South East London (pb)	1-85937-263-5	£9.99
South Somerset	1-85937-318-6	£14.99
South Wales	1-85937-519-7	£14.99
Southampton (pb)	1-85937-427-1	£9.99
Southend (pb)	1-85937-313-5	£9.99
Southport (pb)	1-85937-425-5	£9.99
St Albans (pb)	1-85937-341-0	£9.99
St Ives (pb)	1-85937-415-8	£9.99
Stafford Living Memories (pb)	1-85937-503-0	£9.99
Staffordshire (pb)	1-85937-308-9	£9.99
Stourbridge (pb)	1-85937-530-8	£9.99
Stratford upon Avon (pb)	1-85937-388-7	£9.99
Suffolk (pb)	1-85937-221-x	£9.99
Suffolk Coast (pb)	1-85937-610-x	£9.99
Surrey (pb)	1-85937-240-6	£9.99
Surrey Living Memories	1-85937-328-3	£14.99
Sussex (pb)	1-85937-184-1	£9.99
Sutton (pb)	1-85937-337-2	£9.99
Swansea (pb)	1-85937-167-1	£9.99
Taunton (pb)	1-85937-314-3	£9.99
Tees Valley & Cleveland (pb)	1-85937-623-1	£9.99
Teignmouth (pb)	1-85937-370-4	£7.99
Thanet (pb)	1-85937-116-7	£9.99
Tiverton (pb)	1-85937-178-7	£9.99
Torbay (pb)	1-85937-597-9	£9.99
Truro (pb)	1-85937-598-7	£9.99
Victorian & Edwardian Dorset	1-85937-254-6	£14.99
Victorian & Edwardian Kent (pb)	1-85937-624-X	£9.99
Victorian & Edwardian Maritime Album (pb)	1-85937-622-3	£9.99
Victorian and Edwardian Sussex (pb)	1-85937-625-8	£9.99
Villages of Devon (pb)	1-85937-293-7	£9.99
Villages of Kent (pb)	1-85937-294-5	£9.99
Villages of Sussex (pb)	1-85937-295-3	£9.99
Warrington (pb)	1-85937-507-3	£9.99
Warwick (pb)	1-85937-518-9	£9.99
Warwickshire (pb)	1-85937-203-1	£9.99
Welsh Castles (pb)	1-85937-322-4	£9.99
West Midlands (pb)	1-85937-289-9	£9.99
West Sussex (pb)	1-85937-607-x	£9.99
West Yorkshire (pb)	1-85937-201-5	£9.99
Weston Super Mare (pb)	1-85937-306-2	£9.99
Weymouth (pb)	1-85937-209-0	£9.99
Wiltshire (pb)	1-85937-277-5	£9.99
Wiltshire Churches (pb)	1-85937-171-x	£9.99
Wiltshire Living Memories (pb)	1-85937-396-8	£9.99
Winchester (pb)	1-85937-428-x	£9.99
Windsor (pb)	1-85937-333-x	£9.99
Wokingham & Bracknell (pb)	1-85937-329-1	£9.99
Woodbridge (pb)	1-85937-498-0	£9.99
Worcester (pb)	1-85937-165-5	£9.99
Worcestershire Living Memories	1-85937-489-1	£14.99
Worcestershire	1-85937-152-3	£14.99
York (pb)	1-85937-199-x	£9.99
Yorkshire (pb)	1-85937-186-8	£9.99
Yorkshire Coastal Memories	1-85937-506-5	£14.99
Yorkshire Dales	1-85937-502-2	£14.99
Yorkshire Living Memories (pb)	1-85937-397-6	£9.99

See Frith books on the internet at www.francisfrith.co.uk

FRITH PRODUCTS & SERVICES

Francis Frith would doubtless be pleased to know that the pioneering publishing venture he started in 1860 still continues today. Over a hundred and forty years later, The Francis Frith Collection continues in the same innovative tradition and is now one of the foremost publishers of vintage photographs in the world. Some of the current activities include:

Interior Decoration

Today Frith's photographs can be seen framed and as giant wall murals in thousands of pubs, restaurants, hotels, banks, retail stores and other public buildings throughout the country. In every case they enhance the unique local atmosphere of the places they depict and provide reminders of gentler days in an increasingly busy and frenetic world.

Product Promotions

Frith products are used by many major companies to promote the sales of their own products or to reinforce their own history and heritage. Frith promotions have been used by Hovis bread, Courage beers, Scots Porage Oats, Colman's mustard, Cadbury's foods, Mellow Birds coffee, Dunhill pipe tobacco, Guinness, and Bulmer's Cider.

Genealogy and Family History

As the interest in family history and roots grows world-wide, more and more people are turning to Frith's photographs of Great Britain for images of the towns, villages and streets where their ancestors lived; and, of course, photographs of the churches and chapels where their ancestors were christened, married and buried are an essential part of every genealogy tree and family album.

Frith Products

All Frith photographs are available Framed or just as Mounted Prints and Posters (size 23 x 16 inches). These may be ordered from the address below. From time to time other products - Address Books, Calendars, Table Mats, etc - are available.

The Internet

Already fifty thousand Frith photographs can be viewed and purchased on the internet through the Frith websites and a myriad of partner sites.

For more detailed information on Frith companies and products, look at these sites:

www.francisfrith.co.uk
www.francisfrith.com
(for North American visitors)

See the complete list of Frith Books at:
www.francisfrith.co.uk
This web site is regularly updated with the latest list of publications from the Frith Book Company. If you wish to buy books relating to another part of the country that your local bookshop does not stock, you may purchase on-line.

For further information, trade, or author enquiries please contact us at the address below:
The Francis Frith Collection, Frith's Barn, Teffont, Salisbury, Wiltshire, England SP3 5QP.
Tel: +44 (0)1722 716 376 Fax: +44 (0)1722 716 881 Email: sales@francisfrith.co.uk

See Frith books on the internet at www.francisfrith.co.uk

FREE MOUNTED PRINT

Mounted Print
Overall size 14 x 11 inches

Fill in and cut out this voucher and return *it with your remittance for £2.25 (to cover postage and handling). Offer valid for delivery to UK addresses only.*

Choose any photograph included in this book. *Your SEPIA print will be A4 in size. It will be mounted in a cream mount with a burgundy rule line (overall size 14 x 11 inches).*

Order additional Mounted Prints at HALF PRICE (only £7.49 each*)
If you would like to order more Frith prints from this book, possibly as gifts for friends and family, you can buy them at half price (with no additional postage and handling costs).

Have your Mounted Prints framed
For an extra £14.95 per print* you can have your mounted print(s) framed in an elegant polished wood and gilt moulding, overall size 16 x 13 inches (no additional postage and handling required).

> *** IMPORTANT!**
>
> **These special prices are only available if you order at the same time as you order your free mounted print. You must use the ORIGINAL VOUCHER on this page (no copies permitted). We can only despatch to one address.**

Send completed Voucher form to:
The Francis Frith Collection, Frith's Barn, Teffont, Salisbury, Wiltshire SP3 5QP

CHOOSE ANY IMAGE FROM THIS BOOK

Voucher *for* ***FREE*** *and Reduced Price Frith Prints*

Please do not photocopy this voucher. Only the original is valid, so please fill it in, cut it out and return it to us with your order.

Picture ref no	Page no	Qty	Mounted @ £7.49	Framed + £14.95	Total Cost
		1	Free of charge*	£	£
			£7.49	£	£
			£7.49	£	£
			£7.49	£	£
			£7.49	£	£
			£7.49	£	£
Please allow 28 days for delivery			* Post & handling (UK)		£2.25
			Total Order Cost		£

Title of this book . . . .
I enclose a cheque/postal order for £ . . . .
made payable to 'The Francis Frith Collection'

OR please debit my Mastercard / Visa / Switch / Amex card
(credit cards please on all overseas orders), details below

Card Number

Issue No (Switch only) Valid from (Amex/Switch)

Expires Signature

Name Mr/Mrs/Ms ....
Address ....
....
....
.... Postcode ....
Daytime Tel No ....
Email ....

Valid to 31/12/05

Free Print - see overleaf

Would you like to find out more about Francis Frith?

We have recently recruited some entertaining speakers who are happy to visit local groups, clubs and societies to give an illustrated talk documenting Frith's travels and photographs. If you are a member of such a group and are interested in hosting a presentation, we would love to hear from you.

Our speakers bring with them a small selection of our local town and county books, together with sample prints. They are happy to take orders. A small proportion of the order value is donated to the group who have hosted the presentation. The talks are therefore an excellent way of fundraising for small groups and societies.

Can you help us with information about any of the Frith photographs in this book?

We are gradually compiling an historical record for each of the photographs in the Frith archive. It is always fascinating to find out the names of the people shown in the pictures, as well as insights into the shops, buildings and other features depicted.

If you recognize anyone in the photographs in this book, or if you have information not already included in the author's caption, do let us know. We would love to hear from you, and will try to publish it in future books or articles.

Our production team

Frith books are produced by a small dedicated team at offices in the converted Grade II listed 18th-century barn at Teffont near Salisbury, illustrated above. Most have worked with the Frith Collection for many years. All have in common one quality: they have a passion for the Frith Collection. The team is constantly expanding, but currently includes:

Jason Buck, John Buck, Douglas Mitchell-Burns, Ruth Butler, Heather Crisp, Isobel Hall, Julian Hight, Peter Horne, James Kinnear, Karen Kinnear, Tina Leary, David Marsh, Sue Molloy, Kate Rotondetto, Dean Scource, Eliza Sackett, Terence Sackett, Sandra Sampson, Adrian Sanders, Sandra Sanger, Julia Skinner, Lewis Taylor, Shelley Tolcher and Lorraine Tuck.